OUR DAILY BREAD FOR **KIDS** PRESENTS

Just Teddy

– Learning from Psalm 139 –

By Emily Lim-Leh

Illustrated by Neal Sharp

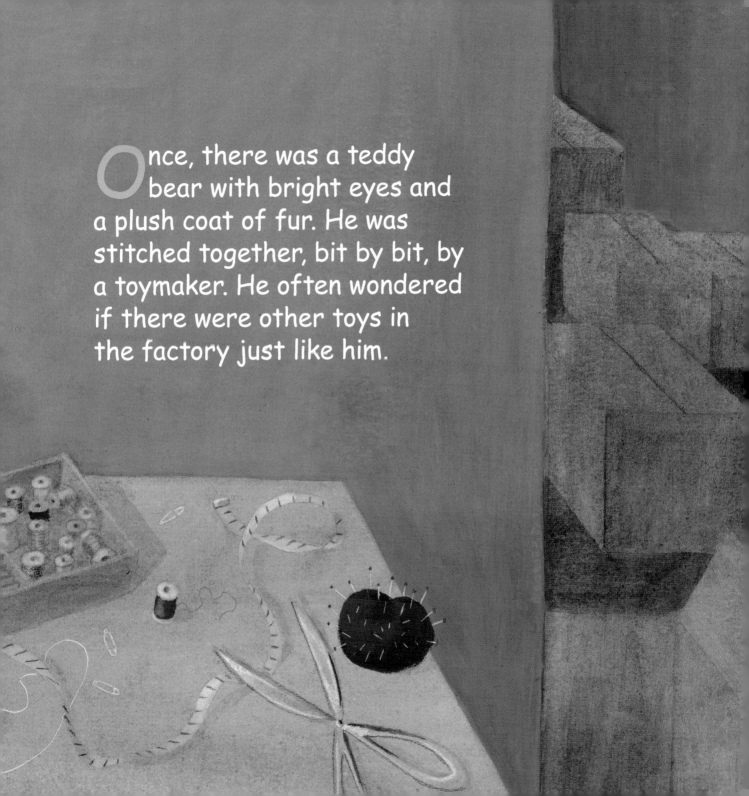

Once, there was a teddy bear with bright eyes and a plush coat of fur. He was stitched together, bit by bit, by a toymaker. He often wondered if there were other toys in the factory just like him.

One evening, after the factory was closed for the day, the bear decided to look around the place. As he climbed down from the table, he tripped and went crashing onto the floor, along with the sewing box. PLINK! PLONK!

"Who's there?" the night watchman shouted. "Oh . . . it's *just* teddy."

The watchman picked up the bear,
tossed him onto a shelf and left.

Several sleepy polar bears were lined up on the shelf.

"You're too wide-eyed to join our
slumber party," one said.

"Your fur coat looks different
from ours," another added.

"Who are *you*?" the polar
bears asked with big yawns.

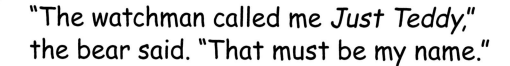

"The watchman called me *Just Teddy*,"
the bear said. "That must be my name."

The polar bears did not hear him. They had fallen fast asleep. *ZzzZzzz*

Just Teddy tried to snuggle with the polar bears, but there was no space for him.

I don't think I fit in here, Just Teddy thought. He climbed down and continued to scout around the factory.

Just Teddy found a group of baby panda bears huddled nearby.

"Where are your black patches?" a panda asked.

Oh no! Just Teddy thought. *The toymaker forgot my patches!*

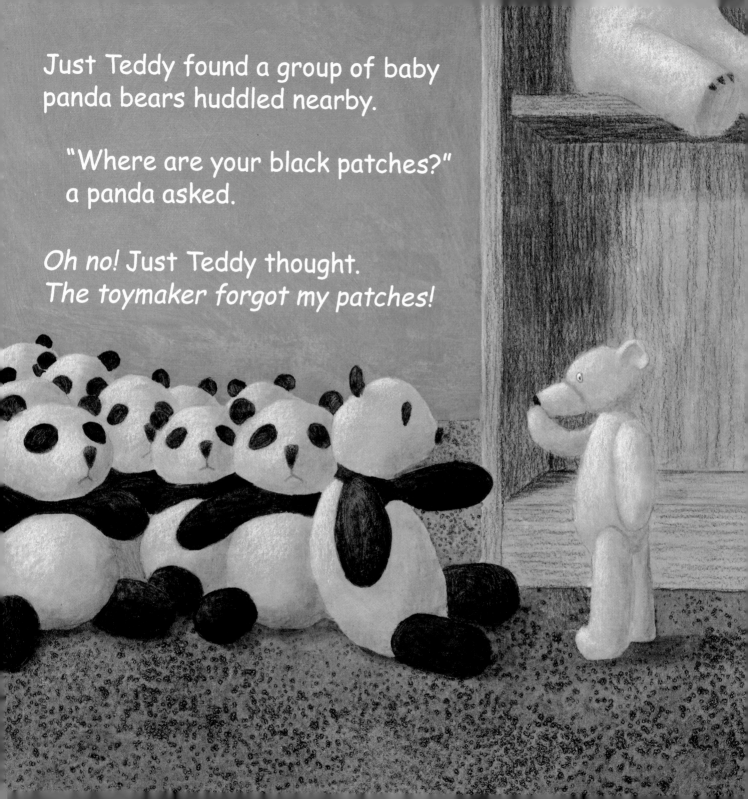

He searched
hard and found a
black marker pen.
Then he hastily
drew dark circles
around his eyes.

SQUIGGLE SQUIGGLE

"What's going on?" a voice cried out from a box nearby. Just Teddy peeped in and saw emperor penguins. He told them what had happened.

"You're welcome to join our party," a penguin said. "Just put on a black tail coat and a white shirt front."

Just Teddy quickly drew himself a black coat, just like the penguins'.

Soon, he was worn out from his adventure and nodded off to sleep.

The next morning, Just Teddy found himself in a toy store.

The shop assistant looked puzzled to find a teddy bear in the penguins' box.

Still, he shoved Just Teddy on
the shelf with the penguins.

PLUNK!

Weeks passed. No one wanted to buy a teddy bear that looked like a cross between a penguin and a panda.

One day, a girl walked by.
She stared at Just Teddy
for some time.

Just Teddy liked her kind face.

"Let's go to the teddy bear shop near our home," the girl's father said. "There will be many bears to choose from."

"But I want this bear," the girl said. "He's special."

She paid for the scruffy bear with her birthday money.

Back home, the girl fussed over Just Teddy.

She tried to read the label on his tummy but it was smudged with ink. She rubbed hard at the label with soap until finally, she saw some numbers.

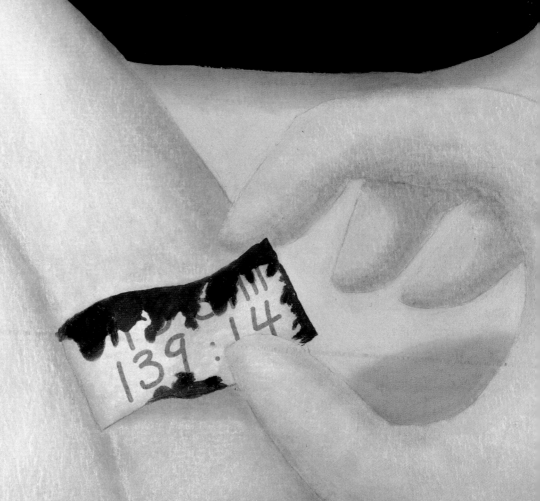

139:14. *I wonder what that means*, she thought.

The girl brought Just Teddy to the teddy bear shop nearby to find out.

The shopkeeper cleaned away most of Just Teddy's ink stains.

SHHHK SHHHK SHHHK

"The label reads 'Psalm 139:14'. It's a Bible verse," the shopkeeper said.

"What does the Bible verse say?" the girl asked.

"No two toys are made the same!

Just leave him here so I have more time to make him squeaky clean."

"No, thanks!" the girl said. Clutching Just Teddy, she skipped home quickly.

"You're not *just* teddy," the girl said. "You're my awesomely made, one-of-a-kind friend!"

So, Just Teddy stopped wondering if there was anyone else like him.

He knew he was uniquely created by his maker and wonderful just the way he was.

"I PRAISE YOU BECAUSE I AM FEARFULLY AND WONDERFULLY MADE; YOUR WORKS ARE WONDERFUL, I KNOW THAT FULL WELL."

—Psalm 139:14 (NIV)

DISCUSSION:

1. Just Teddy wanted so much to be accepted that he tried to become a polar bear, a panda, and a penguin. Have you ever felt like Just Teddy? Have you tried hard to get others to like you?

2. Just Teddy discovers that he is one-of-a-kind with the mark of his maker on his label. God made you a unique, one-of-a-kind person. Think of two or three special things that make you who you are, and praise Him for them!

3. Everyone you meet is someone uniquely created by God. There may be people you like more, and others you like less. No matter what, they are all God's creation. How does knowing that change the way you treat people around you?

4. The Psalms are songs found in the Bible. This means the words in Psalm 139:14 are meant to be song lyrics sung to music! Create your own one-of-a-kind song based on the lyrics found in Psalm 139:14. Teach it to your family and friends.

REFLECTION:

Do you know that you are "fearfully and wonderfully made" by a loving and powerful God? Every one of us is God's special one-of-a-kind creation. God designed us with loving care and detail, and each of us has our own unique traits. We bear the mark of our Creator. Our special label says: "Child of God, awesomely made and greatly valued by God". When others say that you are not "good enough" and "worth less", remember that your God sees you to be of "great worth"! So, let's praise Him! Psalm 139:14 starts with, "I praise you because …" We praise God not only for how He created us, but also for sending His Son, Jesus Christ, to die on the cross for our sins. When we believe in Jesus as our Lord, we gain eternal life (John 3:16). Truly, that's something worthy of high praise!

PRAYER:

Lord, I praise You that I am fearfully and wonderfully made. Help me to see myself as You see me—a special, one-of-a-kind creation with my own unique life purpose. And, help me to praise You for Your creation and for Your salvation through Jesus Christ.

 **YouTube** Watch the *Just Teddy Kids' Sleep Story* on our
@ourdailybreadeurope YouTube channel!